JUSTIN MORNEAU: ALL-STAR BALL STAR

PETER BAILEY

Fenn Publishing Company Ltd.
Bolton, Canada

Fenn Publishing Company Ltd.

JUSTIN MORNEAU: ALL-STAR BALL STAR

A Fenn Publishing Book / First Published in 2008

The content, opinion and subject matter contained herein is the written expression of the author and does not reflect the opinion or ideology of the publisher, or that of the publisher's representatives.

Fenn Publishing Company Ltd.
Bolton, Ontario, Canada
www.hbfenn.com

The publisher gratefully acknowledges the support of the Canada Council for the Arts and the Ontario Arts Council for its publishing program.

We acknowledge the support of the Government of Ontario through the Ontario Media Development Corporation's Ontario Book Initiative.

We acknowledge the financial support of the Government of Canada through the Book Publishing Industry Development Program (BPIDP) for our publishing activities.

Care has been taken to trace ownership of copyright material in this book and to secure permissions. The publishers will gladly receive any information that will enable them to rectify errors or omissions.

Design: First Image
Printed and bound in Canada

Library and Archives Canada Cataloguing in Publication

Bailey, Peter, 1962-
    Justin Morneau : all-star ball star / Peter Bailey.
ISBN 978-1-55168-326-3
    1. Morneau, Justin. 2. Baseball players--Canada--Biography.
3. Minnesota Twins (Baseball team)--Biography. I. Title.

GV865.M67B33 2008   796.357092   C2008-901538-X

CONTENTS

FOREWORD

Justin keeps his eye on the ball and makes solid contact for a base hit.

"In 2006, at the tender age of 25, Justin was named MVP of the AL."

Never before have there been more Canadians in Major League Baseball (MLB) than in 2007 when more than 30 players from "hockey country" appeared in baseball's premier league. Young guns, emerging stars, and established veterans like Jeff Francis, Jason Bay, Eric Gagne, Stubby Clapp, Rich Harden, Adam Loewen, and Russ Martin all contributed to Canada's history in the game, a history that dates back to the late 1800s.

Indeed, the first Canadian to play professionally in the United States was Arthur Irwin, who made his debut in the National League with Worcester in 1880. He was famous for the Irwin glove, a special mitt he produced after breaking two fingers on his catching hand. Not wanting to miss any games, he took a driving glove, added padding, and stitched the fingers together for greater protection and strength.

The first great Canadian star in baseball was the legendary James "Tip" O'Neill. Born in Woodstock, Ontario, he made his debut in 1883 with the New York Gothams of the National League, though he played most of his career with the St. Louis Browns in the American Association. In 1887, O'Neill hit an incredible .435 and became the only player in AA league history to win the Triple Crown – clubbing 14 home runs, recording 225 hits, and driving in 123 runs.

> *Through the years there have been many part-time or fringe players of Canadian birth in MLB, but there have been plenty of stars as well.*

Through the years there have been many part-time or fringe players of Canadian birth in MLB, but there have been plenty of stars as well. Phil Marchildon was a great player with Philadelphia in the American League in the 1940s, and, of course, Ferguson Jenkins had a hall of fame career from 1965 to 1983.

More recently, British Columbia's Dave McKay played for the Blue Jays, as did Paul Quantrill (born London, Ontario), and in 2003 relief pitcher Eric Gagne won the Cy Young Award for his spectacular season in which he converted every save opportunity, the only pitcher ever to be 100% perfect over a full season. His 62 straight saves is a record, and he is the only reliever to have more than 50 saves in two seasons (he had exactly 50 in 2002).

Of course, it's impossible to mention Canada and baseball without celebrating the career of Larry Walker, another B.C. native. He won seven Gold Glove awards for his outstanding defensive play in right field. He also won three batting titles in the National League; and, in 1997, he was named the most valuable player of the NL, the first Canadian so honoured.

Larry Walker

It is not surprising that another B.C. native, Justin Morneau, became the first Canadian in the American League to match Walker's greatest accomplishment. In 2006, at the tender age of 25, Justin was named MVP of the AL for his season which included a .321 batting average, 34 home runs, and 130 runs batted in, with the Minnesota Twins. His rise to greatness was swift, but it was not unexpected. This is his story, the story of Justin Morneau's life in baseball.

Relief pitcher Eric Gagne had a perfect season with the Dodgers in 2003.

CHAPTER ONE

AS A BOY IN BRITISH COLUMBIA

Justin slides safely into home plate.

"I still think about what might have happened if I had gone and played hockey."

Justin

Justin Morneau was born in New Westminster, British Columbia, not far from Vancouver, in 1981. His dad, George, had lived in New Westminster all his life, and his mom, Audra, was born in Medicine Hat, Alberta. When she was young her family moved to Victoria, B.C. which is on an island just off the coast of the mainland.

When Audra got older she attended the University of Victoria with the intention of becoming a schoolteacher. She had five siblings, all boys, so grew up athletically inclined. In particular, Audra excelled at softball. She was a great hitter and equally skilled as a pitcher. When in university, she joined a softball team for fun, and the team's coach was none other than George Morneau. They got along well, and in 1976 they were married.

The happy couple settled in New Westminster, and because they wanted a family Audra left university to settle down. They had one child, Geordie, who was born on November 14, 1979. He was named after George, whose nickname was Geordie. Less than two years later, on May 15, 1981, they had another son. They named him Justin Ernest George Morneau.

Never before have there been more Canadians in Major League Baseball (MLB) than in 2007

Both mom and dad encouraged the kids to be physically active from an early age. By the time Justin was just two years old, he and his brother were playing waffle ball in their backyard. Waffle ball is baseball with a light plastic ball that has holes in it. This ball never traveled very far and could not injure anyone or break windows, but Geordie and Justin could still throw it or hit it with all of their might.

Two years later, Justin's obsession with waffle ball was still strong, so his dad bought him an electronic waffle ball pitching machine. The machine allowed Justin to stand in a homemade batter's box and hit balls delivered from the machine. Of course, because waffle balls had holes, the ball's flight was never consistent and it was difficult to hit these "waffling" balls. In truth, Justin was actually learning to hit curve balls, change-ups, and knuckle balls from the time he was four years old!

A few years later, another important development in the family occurred. Justin's dad came home one day and declared that he was sick of his job. He quit and bought a store! He was going to run a sporting goods business. For Justin and Geordie, this was like a dream come true. Imagine a store with every kind of sports equipment you could want—hockey sticks and skates, baseball gloves, footballs, tennis racquets. You name it; the store was going to sell it.

> *Imagine a store with every kind of sports equipment you could want— hockey sticks and skates, baseball gloves, footballs, tennis racquets.*

Of course, the kids thought this was their own private department store, but, in fact, it was something outside the store that was of far more interest to Justin and Geordie than anything their dad had on the shelves. In the back lot behind the store was a batting cage, the same as the waffle-ball machine but an adult version, almost the genuine baseball version!

This batting machine threw fastballs, not waffle balls. This was important for two reasons. One, fastballs are smaller and are what pro players in Major League Baseball use. And, two, this machine threw the ball faster, resembling MLB baseball all the more. Justin used to spend his whole Sundays in the batting cage. His dad used to tell him all the time to use, "fast hands," to hit. By that he meant that Justin had to get the bat moving quickly, be prepared to hit the ball and be in the swinging motion before the ball left the pitcher's hand. Fast hands meant staying "on top" of the ball and being in a position to drive the ball to all parts of the ballpark. Slow hands meant slow reaction, and this meant either a foul ball or, as play-by-play announcers like say, "a swing and a miss."

Justin stretches and loosens up before a game.

When he got older and wanted the real experience, Justin went to other places for batting practice. In truth, he became totally obsessed by the batting cage. It was such a fun place to hit the ball hard, to practice his swing, and to learn how to "see" the ball as it left the automatic "arm" of the machine and delivered a pitch. "Justin used to go to the batting cages and his hands would bleed," his dad recalled later. "He'd say, 'Dad, you got some tape so I can tape my hands up?' I'd tape him up and he'd keep on hitting, even though his hands were bleeding. He'd hit 300 balls off the tee, and 200 live [from the pitching machine], every day."

> I'd tape him up and he'd keep on hitting, even though his hands were bleeding.

Justin was not only a fanatic about baseball. Like most Canadian boys, he loved hockey, and his hero was Patrick Roy, which is why Justin wears number 33, the same number that "Saint Patrick" wore with the Montreal Canadiens and Colorado Avalanche when he won four Stanley Cups. Justin played as much road hockey in the summer as baseball, and in the winter he was developing into a fine prospect on ice—as a goalie, of course. He also wore number 33 on his hockey teams! When his mom drove him to games, he refused to leave the car until the clock read ":33" in the minutes column (i.e., 6:33 am or 7:33 am), such was his love for Patrick Roy and his obsession with Roy's number 33!

This baseball-hockey combination earned Justin athlete of the year honours at New Westminster Secondary School one year. In addition to these two sports, Justin also loved skateboarding and basketball, and it was in part because of this mix of sports that he became such a great athlete. No matter what sport you love the most, it's never good to play only one sport. In Justin's case, for instance, skateboarding was very helpful for developing his balance, a key to being a successful batter, as well as leg strength and coordination. Basketball

Justin helped Canada qualify for the 2006 Summer Olympics.

The classic powerful swing of Justin Morneau—great balance, eyes on the ball, perfect execution.

Justin Morneau: All-Star Ball Star

helped his jumping muscles, important for any baseball player in the field, as well as for timing.

Northern Secondary didn't have a baseball team, so Justin ended up playing for an amateur team called the North Delta Blue Jays. At this time Justin was a catcher, and the star pitcher was Jeff Francis. Jeff went on to play for the Colorado Rockies and pitched in the 2007 World Series. It's really quite amazing that both Jeff and Justin, two of the greatest stars in baseball today, both got their starts on the same small team in British Columbia, a province not exactly known for developing star ball players!

It was during his time with North Delta that Justin (like Jeff) started to receive serious consideration from MLB scouts. The great duo of Jeff and Justin led the Blue Jays to national championship titles in both 1997 and 1998, and Justin was named the best catcher and hitter in the league in '98. Justin graduated from high school the next year, in the spring of 1999. On June 2, 1999, he was drafted by the Minnesota Twins.

I still think about what might have happened if I had gone and played hockey, but it was one of those things...

"That was a really tough decision," Justin said years later. "I still think about what might have happened if I had gone and played hockey, but it was one of those things...It was an easy decision at the time because I had such a good summer playing baseball. It was either go off and play hockey and leave home when I was 16 or 17, and I don't think I was ready for that yet." Although he had attended the training camp of the Portland Winter Hawks of the Western Hockey League, the future goalie "retired" so the future ball player could start a career on the diamond.

And so, on June 17, 1999, Justin Ernest George Morneau of New Westminster, British Columbia, signed his first professional baseball contract. Justin's hockey days were over, but his life as a pro baseball player was just beginning.

CHAPTER TWO

PURSUING A DREAM

Justin is tagged out at third base by Boston's Bill Mueller.

"Quick hands, Justin!
Quick hands!"

Justin's father, George

Once a player is drafted at age 18, the difference between baseball and hockey is huge. In hockey, a star player can make the NHL in his first year. Sometimes, he'll go back to junior and make the NHL the year after, or he may go to the minors for two or three years. In baseball, the process is much slower, much more gradual, and requires a lot more patience from the player. For starters, there are so many more levels of play. You start off in a Rookie League, then play in an A league ("A ball" it's called), then AA ("double A"), then AAA ("triple A"), and then the big leagues. And even then, there are in-between leagues like A- and A+.

As soon as Justin was drafted, he focused entirely on making it to the major leagues. So, the first step for him was spending a summer in Rookie League. And, since he was now in the Minnesota system, the first stop was a team called the GCL Twins of the Gulf Coast League, a team that played in Fort Myers, Florida. Justin later called this town "Fort Misery" because playing conditions were horrible. Games were scheduled for high noon under the beating sun with temperatures so hot it felt like the bat was going to melt in his hands. There were no fans to speak of in the stands, but fortunately the season was nearly over by the time he got there. Justin played in only 17 games in the summer of 1999, but had a .302 batting average, a good sign for a brief introduction to the pro game.

As soon as Justin was drafted, he focused entirely on making it to the major leagues.

The next year, the year 2000, Justin played the full season at Fort Misery, and although conditions were no better his performance was hotter than the sun and more spectacular than the reflection from the empty seats. Justin hit .402 and became an all-star, ensuring his days in the Rookie League were quickly over. At the end of the season, he was sent to the Elizabethton Twins as a ringer (i.e., a very good player in a not very good league). This team also played in a Rookie League, and Justin got there just in time to help Elizabethton win a championship.

It was during this season that Justin made the transition that would be the first step on his road to an all-star career in the major leagues. Up until now, he had always been a catcher—which was the baseball position that most closely mirrored a hockey goalie—but the team had another excellent prospect as a catcher and asked Justin to move to first base. Although there aren't many first basemen who catch with their right hand, Justin made the adjustment and in the process probably added years to his pro career. (Catchers, with all their squatting, often develop knee problems and don't play as long as other fielders.)

> *What Justin was in the process of doing was the same thing that all great players before him or after him do—they improve as the level of competition improves.*

The next year, 2001, Justin started his ascent through the formal levels of baseball. He joined the Quad City River Bandits, an A level team in the Midwest League, but by the time this season was over, he had jumped two levels of play and was making a very quick run to Major League Baseball and 50,000-seat ballparks. Justin hit a remarkable .356 for Quad City and had 53 runs batted in (RBIs) in just 64 games. Every at bat he took, every time he focused on his swing, he started by thinking of his dad's words: "Quick hands, Justin! Quick hands!"

His performance at the A level earned him a promotion to the Florida State League, an A+ level of play located where he played Rookie League ball. In fact, Justin was assigned to the Fort Myers Miracle, a team right back in "Fort Misery." In 53 games, he was only slightly less impressive than in Quad City, hitting .294 and producing 40 RBIs in 53 games.

What Justin was in the process of doing was the same thing that all great players before him or after him do—they improve as the level of competition improves. For every promotion

Justin pops the ball in the air.

New York Yankees' shortstop Derek Jeter watches Justin round the bases after hitting a home run.

Justin earned, for every league he played in that had better pitching, better hitting, better fielding, Justin was able to excel and improve on his own performance. As a result, he received one more promotion this season, going to the New Britain Rock Cats of the Eastern League, a team in "double A" ball. He had only six hits in 38 at-bats, but this was only in the final ten days of the season.

His rapid progress over the course of just one season assured Justin a place back with New Britain the following year. In 2002, for the first time, he played the entire season in one place, and he again learned by leaps and bounds. And, now 21 years old, his body was filling out. Justin grew to be 6'4", and he added plenty of muscle on what was once a scrawny body in Rookie League just three years previous.

It was both an honour and a good sign that others saw him as one of the top prospects in the game.

Although Justin hit an excellent .298 for New Britain in 2002, the most important part of the season came during the All-Star break for Major League Baseball. Just a few years earlier, MLB had started the Futures Game, a game held prior to the MLB All-Star Game and featuring the top players from the minors. Many up-and-coming stars of MLB had played in this game during its brief, three-year history, and Justin was named to the team in '02. It was both an honour and a good sign that others saw him as one of the top prospects in the game. As a result, he got to be around the big boys of the Yankees, Red Sox, Dodgers, and Blue Jays for a couple of days. He watched how they hit the ball; he talked to them about playing; and, he took in the experience of the highest level of play.

His performance in AA ball in 2002 led to an invitation to the Minnesota Twins' spring training camp in March 2003. There was no way Justin was going to make the team, but again it was the experience that counted most. The team felt it would give Justin a taste of the real pro game so that he would feel motivated to go back to the minors and focus all the more on his dream of reaching MLB. What the Twins hadn't counted on, though, was just how impressive Justin's training camp was going to be! In eight games, he hit .429 and had ten RBIs. More important, he showed no signs of being intimidated by the big stars or unable to compete at this level.

Justin was sent back to New Britain for the remainder of 2003, but he lasted only 20 games. He hit the ball too well and was clearly better than the league he was in. At this stage in his career, he needed to be pushed and challenged, not starring in a minor league. So, he was promoted to the Rochester Red Wings, Minnesota's Triple-A (AAA) affiliate in the International League. This was the last step before the majors. As he had proved everywhere else, Justin made the adjustment with the ease of a star in the making. Although his average was only .268 over 71 games, he hit the ball well and, more impressively, had developed a power to his skill at the plate. He hit 16 home runs in 265 at-bats, and given his ability to adjust quickly, there was only one thing the Twins could do with him—call him up.

> *"I ended up out on the street in my uniform in Buffalo talking on my cell phone!"*

On June 9, 2003, Justin and his Rochester teammates were in Buffalo for a game against the Bisons. While he was at batting practice, working on his hitting, his manager, Phil Roof, told him to call the Minnesota Twins. Their first baseman, Chris Gomez, had suffered an injury, and they needed a replacement. Justin tells the story, "As soon as I got done in the [batting] cage, I ran and got my cell phone, but I couldn't get a signal anywhere. I ended up out on the street in my uniform in Buffalo talking on my cell phone!"

A day later, Justin was in Minneapolis, Minnesota. He was about to play in his first Major League Baseball game.

Nick Punto (#8) congratulates Justin after a home run.

CHAPTER THREE

THE CANADIAN TRADITION

"When you go to other cities, and
you see other Canadian guys, it's
like you already know them."

Justin

Justin was to become part of Canadian sports history, but in time his name would become more important than just a name on a list of Canadians to play in MLB. Indeed, he was about to start a career that was of historic importance to baseball in Canada. Before him, dozens of Canadians had made it to the big leagues, and many of those players had made an excellent impression.

Canadians have been playing major league baseball since the very beginning of the game. The first was Bill Philipps, who was born in Saint John, New Brunswick and started in 1879 with Cleveland. Philipps, however, was raised in Chicago, Illinois. The first superstar who was truly Canadian was James "Tip" O'Neill. He played from 1883 to 1892, but 1887 will go down as one of the greatest years by any player in any era. He had a .435 batting average that year and set a record for hits (225), doubles (52), slugging percentage (.691), and total bases (357). The batting average was second highest all-time (Hugh Duffy hit .440 in 1894).

Before him, dozens of Canadians had made it to the big leagues ...

Another early star from Canada was Bob Emslie. Born in Guelph, Ontario, Bob won 32 games pitching for the Baltimore Orioles in 1885. Another pitcher, Russ Ford, won 26 games for the New York Highlanders in 1910. John Hiller was also a pitcher of note, but from the modern era. In 1973, he saved a then-record 38 games, and the following season he set a record with 17 wins as a relief pitcher. Dick Fowler has the distinction of being the only Canadian pitcher to throw a no-hitter, a feat he accomplished on September 9, 1945, pitching for the Athletics over the Browns.

Another extraordinary story was provided by Ron Taylor. Today, he is a renowned doctor in Toronto, but in the 1960s he was a great relief pitcher. He won two World Series, one in 1964 with the St. Louis Cardinals, the second five years later with the

"Miracle Mets" in New York. What made Taylor's achievements more remarkable was that in six post-season games (four of which were World Series games), he never allowed a single earned run! That's right—his career playoff ERA is 0.00!

Two players, however, tower over all other Canadians—pitcher Ferguson "Fergie" Jenkins and right fielder Larry Walker. Jenkins is the only Canadian inducted into the National Baseball Hall of Fame in Cooperstown, New York. He is the only pitcher in major league baseball history to have recorded at least 3,000 strikeouts (3,192) and walked fewer than 1,000 players (997).

Two players, however, tower over all other Canadians—pitcher Ferguson "Fergie" Jenkins and right fielder Larry Walker.

More important, though, Fergie put together six straight 20-win seasons with the Chicago Cubs, something that hasn't been done since the 1950s. His 1971 season was one of the best in modern baseball history. He won 24 games, pitched 325 innings, and had an incredible 30 complete games. He also played errorless ball for four straight years, a National League record. Between 1967 and 1980, he won 251 games, more than any other pitcher in the majors, and by the time he retired, he was second all-time in strikeouts. There was no question he was destined to be a hall of famer!

The same will probably be said for Larry Walker in the coming years. He retired only in 2005, so he won't be eligible to be inducted into the hall of fame until 2011. Nevertheless, his career certainly merits induction when the time comes. Larry was born in British Columbia, not far from Justin Morneau, and from 1989 to 2005 he was one of the best hitters and fielders in all of baseball. He played in 1,988 games, more than any other Canadian, and he is among that rare group of players to have a lifetime batting average over .300 (.313).

Without question, Larry's "career year" was 1997 when he was named the National League's most valuable player.

Fergie Jenkins is honoured with a plaque on the Walk of Fame in downtown Toronto in 2001.

That season, he hit 49 home runs, drove in 130 runs, and had an average of .366. He even stole 33 bases to join the very exclusive 30-30 club (30 home runs and 30 stolen bases in the same year), to indicate both his great power at the plate and speed on the basepaths. In all, Larry finished first in 12 statistical categories in 1997. He also played in five All-Star Games and earned seven Gold Glove awards for his play in right field during his exceptional career.

Justin Morneau is now part of this pantheon of Canadian players in major league baseball, and he is playing in an age of unprecedented participation by Canadians. In 2006, there were some 23 Canadians in MLB, the most since 1884. In 2007, that number shot past 30. More important, many of the modern Canadians are not fringe players but stars on their team and in the league.

> "When you go to other cities, and you see other Canadian guys, it's like you already know them, even if you've never met."

For instance, there is Jason Bay, the outstanding left fielder with Pittsburgh. Baltimore pitcher Eric Bedard is one of the finest young throwers in the game. Ryan Dempster and Jeff Francis (Chicago Cubs and Colorado Rockies) are also star pitchers, and Eric Gagne (Milwaukee) won the Cy Young Award in 2003 with the Los Angeles Dodgers after saving all 52 chances, a major league record. Russell Martin of the Dodgers in considered the best young catcher in the game.

Other top names in the game include Rich Harden, Shawn Hill, Corey Koskie, Adam Loewen, Scott Mathieson, Pete Orr, Matt Stairs, Mark Teahen, and Scott Thorman. In truth, Canadians might not dominate the game, but there is at least one star player at virtually every position, meaning that the next time a World Baseball Classic event happens (in the spring of 2009), don't be surprised to see Canada battling for the championship along with Cuba and Japan!

Baltimore Orioles' left-handed pitcher Erik Bedard is one of many star Canadians in baseball in 2008.

Justin enjoys the friendship shared among the Canadian players in the game, even if he doesn't know each one personally. "There's camaraderie among the Canadian players," he said. "When you go to other cities, and you see other Canadian guys, it's like you already know them, even if you've never met." Indeed, they all end up meeting each other and saying hello simply because they share a common and strong bond—their home and native land.

CHAPTER FOUR

THE
FIRST GAME

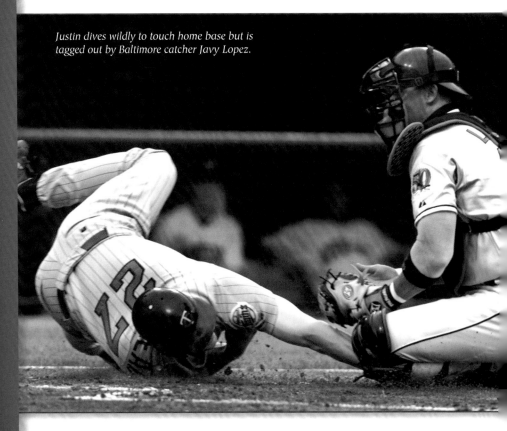

Justin dives wildly to touch home base but is tagged out by Baltimore catcher Javy Lopez.

"Justin's potential is unlimited."

Coach Al Newman

All the details of Justin's first game will stay with him forever. The day after being called up, he had to wake up really early to catch his flight to Minneapolis. He arrived at the ball park very early, met the coaching staff, and went to his hotel to rest. He returned to the ballpark well before the game to meet his teammates. It was then he shook hands with manager Ron Gardenhire who told Justin that he would be playing that night. Justin would be the team's designated hitter (in other words, he would bat but not play in the field). He would be batting fourth, the key position in the lineup. The player with power and the ability to drive in runs always bats fourth, which is why that position is often called batting "clean up." That's the player who dominates and clears the bases of all runners with one great hit.

If all of this wasn't amazing enough, Justin was further excited because the Twins were playing the Colorado Rockies, a team that featured Larry Walker, another player from British Columbia and possibly the greatest baseball player ever born in Canada. Larry had always been Justin's hero, and to make his major-league debut in Larry's presence was like a rookie lining up for a faceoff against Wayne Gretzky in his first game. During batting practice, Larry said hello to Justin and wished him well. Moments later, he sent Justin a signed bat with three important words on it: "Make Canada proud." Justin was thrilled and honoured by the gesture. That night Justin got a photo of himself, Larry, and another Canadian player, Corey Koskie, standing behind home plate, which is a cherished memento for Justin from that first game.

> *The day after being called up, he had to wake up really early to catch his flight to Minneapolis.*

There was an even more important person at the ballpark this day than Larry Walker, though. As soon as he heard the news about being called up the previous day, Justin called his father and told him the spectacular news. And so, soon after the gates opened to let fans in, George Morneau made his way to his seat to watch his son play in the big leagues, the same son who at age two played waffle ball in the family's backyard in New Westminster, British Columbia!

The Twins were out 1-2-3 in the first inning, so Justin's first at-bat came at the start of the bottom of the second inning. He was facing right-handed pitcher Jason Jennings, which was good for Justin, who bats left. It's always easier for a batter to face a pitcher who throws opposite to the side you hit because the angle of the ball to the plate favours the batter.

... Justin's first at-bat came at the start of the bottom of the second inning.

The first pitch was a ball. The second pitch was right over the plate and Justin took a mighty swing. He hit a foul ball that soared off the roof of the Metrodome. Although it was only another strike in just another game, the distance the ball traveled had fans ooohing and aaahing with excitement. Justin watched another ball miss the strike zone before lining another foul ball down the right field line. With the count 2-2 (two balls, two strikes), Justin made perfect contact on the fifth pitch and drove the ball up the middle for a solid single in his first at-bat! The crowd gave him a standing ovation, and the team collected the ball for Justin to take home to his parents. "It helped me relax more," he admitted afterwards about the first hit. "It took a weight off my shoulders—it felt good!"

"I was just tickled pink!" his dad, George, beamed. "I was probably more excited than him. I told him I was coming... seeing my boy up at bat, getting a hit his first time up, and everybody giving him a standing ovation. I started crying." The day had also been special for Justin's dad because he had become friends with Larry Walker's dad, so to see his son talking to Larry down on the field was unbelievable.

Justin takes a mighty cut at home plate.

Jason Jennings was the first pitcher Justin faced
in the majors, and he got a hit off the big right-hander.

Justin Morneau: All-Star Ball Star

Justin didn't fare so well in his next at bat, but in the sixth inning he drove another hard ball to right field for his second hit of the night. In the eighth inning, he had to bat against a left-handed pitcher, Brian Fuentes, and again he was put out. The Twins lost the game, 5-0, but Justin went 2-for-4 in his major league debut. Incredibly, only one other player for Minnesota got a hit that night.

In the dressing room after the game, the "kid" was surrounded by reporters and, as has become tradition in baseball, this meant that while he was being interviewed Justin was going to have his face smeared with whipped cream! He wiped his face as reporters smiled and photographers took pictures, but he continued fielding questions until all reporters had had all the information they required. Day One as a pro baseball player was officially over, and Justin walked out of the Metrodome with his dad, exhilarated and exhausted.

> *Day One as a pro baseball player was officially over, and Justin walked out of the Metrodome with his dad ...*

George has become the family archivist and has several mementoes from Justin's career, starting with the ball from his first pro hit, the first bat for a home run, the first ball from the game the previous evening, and then one more amazing memory—the lineup card. One of the Minnesota coaches had the team sign it, and then Larry Walker got everyone on Colorado to sign it before giving it to Justin and his dad. Needless to say, that card became one priceless memento in the Morneau household.

Of course, one game does not make a career, and Justin had another game to play the next day. He was again the DH (designated hitter), and again he was batting clean-up. Justin continued to swing the bat well. "Fast hands." In the bottom of the first inning, with runners on first base and second base and only one out, Justin drilled another pitch to right field. The hit scored one runner to give the Twins an early 1-0 lead

Corey Koskie (#47) was an important teammate to Justin during the early years of his career.

and Justin had his first RBI. In the third inning, he was walked intentionally so that the pitcher—right-hander Aaron Cook—could face a right-handed batter in a tense situation, and in the fifth inning Justin was at it again. He had another base hit and scored later in the inning on a wild pitch, marking his first run scored in the big leagues.

Third-base coach Al Newman (#62) was also the team's batting coach and an integral part of Justin's development as a hitter.

In the sixth inning, Justin hit a long fly ball out that almost made it over the fence for his first home run, and in the eighth inning he got his third hit of the night with an infield single. More important for his place on the team, the Twins won the game, 7-4. In two games, Justin had five hits in eight at-bats, a .625 average. As he said to everyone afterwards, "There's nowhere to go but down now. It's fun, but not every day is going to be like that."

One of his coaches, Al Newman, who managed Justin back in the Rookie League in 1999, saw things differently. "Justin's potential is unlimited, and with his work ethic, I'm sure he'll continue to progress."

CHAPTER FIVE

THE NEXT STAGE

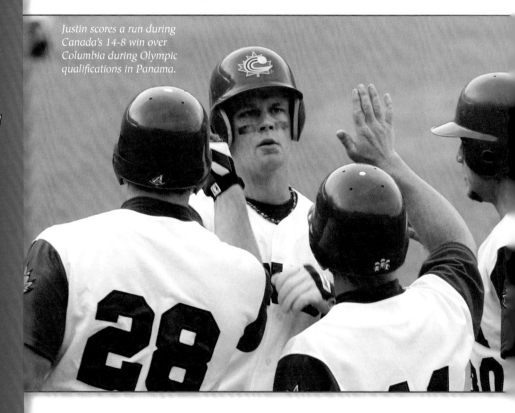

Justin scores a run during Canada's 14-8 win over Columbia during Olympic qualifications in Panama.

"I don't expect to see Justin Morneau back here this season."

Phil Roof, minor-league coach

Justin did, indeed, progress, but at a slow and steady pace, not all in one day or one week. He stayed with the team for the better part of two months, but his batting average settled in comfortably under .300 and he didn't play every day. Indeed, his manager, Ron Gardenhire, tried to maximize Justin's performance by playing him mostly against right-handed pitchers or late in a game when the outcome had already been decided. Justin learned a little bit more each day he was in the majors, but with fewer at-bats than he was used to, his swing got a little rusty and he went into a bit of a slump.

He hit his first home run on June 17, late in a game against Kansas City during a bad 14-7 loss, but he had only two multiple-hit games the rest of his stay with the team. By the time he was sent back to Triple-A, Justin was batting only .227 and had only four hits in his most recent 37 plate appearances. He did hit four homers, though, and two of them—one in Milwaukee, one in Detroit—were the longest home runs in those cities by anyone all year long. In fact, his blast at Miller Park in Milwaukee was measured at 460 feet, the longest to date in that park's history! And, all four homers came in his first 43 times in the batter's box. He was not only a batter who could hit the ball consistently all over the park; he could also drive the ball a long, long way, a quality Minnesota had been lacking for many years.

> *They knew he was going to be a great player, but they also knew he needed a bit more time developing.*

Justin's slump didn't matter to the Twins, though. They knew he was going to be a great player, but they also knew he needed a bit more time developing. Justin went back to Rochester with a positive attitude, and in September when teams are allowed to expand their rosters, Justin was called up again. "I wasn't playing that much at the end," he said of his demotion in late July. "I'd get in a game and think I'd have to hit a home run every at bat. I started chasing pitches I wouldn't normally swing at. I'd start thinking, 'If I hit a home run here, I'll be in the lineup tomorrow.' I was ready to start playing every day again," he admitted.

When Justin was called up in September, he again played only sporadically and in certain situations, but he was part of an important experience nonetheless. The Twins were a team fighting for a spot in the playoffs, so although Justin wasn't on the field every day, he got to experience what playoff pressure was all about and how he should deal with a tight pennant race.

He hit a home run in five straight games, and Canada did, indeed, advance to the Olympics!

By the end of the year, Justin wasn't ready to play every day in the majors, but he had certainly made important strides since the start of training camp. "I feel like I've come a long way this year," he said, "but I need to play more at first base, see more pitchers, and get more at-bats."

Once the major league season was over, Justin kept right on playing. He joined Team Canada in Panama to help it qualify for the 2004 Olympics in Athens, Greece, and although the trip didn't receive much publicity back home, Justin's performance was unbelievable. He hit a home run in five straight games, and Canada did, indeed, advance to the Olympics! "It was an awesome feeling," he said later. "We had a great team and a lot of fun. It's one of those things I'll probably never be able to duplicate."

After this successful trip, Justin then played "winter ball," a league run in the Dominican Republic, a country that has hot, sunny weather at a time of year when much of North America is covered in snow. He then spent part of the off-season training with the Twins' regular first baseman, Doug Mientkiewicz, before finally taking a few weeks off.

Canada's Pierre Laforest high-fives Justin after a homer against Mexico during Olympic qualifications.

The other half of the M & M boys, Joe Mauer delivers a big hit.

By the time the 2004 season rolled around, Justin was an even better player than when the previous big-league season had ended. As in 2003, Justin started the season by attending the Twins' spring training camp and performing well in exhibition games during the so-called "grapefruit league." Again, Justin started the year with Rochester in the International League, but this time the Twins called him up in late May after he had an impressive start that year in Triple-A. But again, this was a promotion only because Minnesota's regular catcher, Joe Mauer, was placed on the disabled list. Justin played only seven games with the Twins this time, and he returned to Rochester when Joe was healthy, but when he was back with the Red Wings, Justin resumed hitting for power and had a batting average the Twins simply couldn't ignore.

By the time the 2004 season rolled around, Justin was an even better player...

Justin was called up in mid-July and started to play full games, every day. His manager in Rochester, Phil Roof, spoke plainly of the promotion this time: "I don't expect to see Justin Morneau back here this season." Phil couldn't have been more correct. Just two weeks after Justin joined the Twins this time, something happened that changed his life and career. On July 31, 2004, the Twins traded their star first baseman, Doug Mientkiewicz, to Boston. The message was absolutely clear. The Twins had a first baseman already—Justin—and they didn't need Doug any longer!

Some fans were shocked by the trade because Justin was still pretty little known and Doug Mientkiewicz was a star. But the Twins assured everyone that soon—very soon—they would forget about Doug because Justin was going to play just as well. Of course, Justin was happy to receive such a confidence boost from management, but he was also a little bit nervous because he had to play like a major league first baseman. He now had to learn and perform at the same time. He knew if he didn't play well fans would boo him and he'd feel even more pressure to perform. Yet, as every great player does, and as Justin had done throughout his career, every move up had little effect on his ability to play like a star. Indeed, the great players always, as they say, rise to the occasion.

There might have been another reason for Minnesota making the big trade by July 31. That was the date all teams in MLB had to make an important decision: any player who was on the team's roster on July 31 could not play for his country at the 2004 Summer Olympics. The Twins knew Justin would be chosen to play for Canada, but by making the trade they put him on their roster before midnight of the end of July and ensured he wasn't going anywhere.

Had Justin been with the team, a gold medal would not have been out of the question.

On the one hand, Justin was sad for the missed opportunity to play for his country at the greatest show on earth; on the other hand, he was now a full-time baseball player in the majors. Interestingly, Canada played extremely well in Athens, losing the bronze-medal game to Japan and finishing in fourth place. Had Justin been with the team, a gold medal would not have been out of the question.

So Justin remained in the majors the rest of the year. He played 74 games for Minnesota in 2004, and he had a batting average of .271. He clobbered 19 home runs and drove in 58 runs in just 280 at-bats, numbers that would be amazing if he could keep that same pace over a full season. In all, he hit 41 home runs and had 121 RBIs in Triple-A and MLB combined, a pretty impressive total. Justin was now 6'4" and weighed 230 pounds thanks to a careful regimen of exercise, training, and diet. He wasn't just a skilled player—he was a force when he stepped in the batter's box.

Justin's focus and intensity have been of tremendous help in getting him to the top of baseball.

Justin rounds the bases like he's done dozens of times before.

More important, Justin's own efforts helped his team. The Twins were a serious contender for the championship when he started to play full-time in mid-July, and thanks to Justin's power, he helped the team get into the playoffs. The Twins won the American League Central Division title by nine games and were on their way to the post-season. "Last year, I kind of felt on the outside looking in," Justin said of Minnesota's success in 2003. "I didn't feel like I contributed much to it. This year, I've been playing every day from the All-Star break on, so I feel like I actually had something to do with it."

As well, his experience from last year's pennant race in September had been vital to his fine play this year. "Being around last year, seeing how everyone acted, and the atmosphere and that kind of stuff helped me to be more relaxed this time around," he admitted. In fact, when Justin returned to the Twins on July 15, he had a .250 batting average up to that point of the year. By the time the regular season had ended and the team had won its division, Justin's average was .271. In other words, as the action got more fierce and competitive, Justin played better and better—and he still hadn't played a full season in the majors yet.

> *This year, I've been playing every day from the All-Star break on, so I feel like I actually had something to do with it."*

The Twins' post-season was too short for their liking. The New York Yankees eliminated Minnesota in four games in the best-of-five series, and Justin had only four hits in 17 at-bats. Nevertheless, it was a good first taste of the playoffs for him, and he headed into the off season with tremendous confidence. At the next training camp, in February 2005, he was set to be the team's number-one first baseman, and he was still batting in the powerful fourth spot – cleanup. Justin's career was now set to move full steam ahead.

A ROUGH TIME

CHAPTER SIX

Justin uses great speed and excellent technique to beat the tag.

"I've struggled more than I'd like to, but I've learned from it."

Justin

I f 2005, was supposed to be a breakout year for Justin, it wasn't. Almost as soon as 2004 had ended, things started to go wrong for him. He had to have his appendix removed before Christmas, and soon after the surgery and recovery he suffered chicken pox, pneumonia, and pleurisy. As a result, he arrived in spring training in less than 100 percent perfect condition. Then, on April 6, in a game against Seattle, Justin was hit in the head by a pitch from Ron Villone. The ball hit both the corner of his helmet and his bare skull, and Justin crashed to the ground in agony.

Justin suffered a concussion, but thankfully he wasn't seriously injured. Although he missed only 16 playing days, the long-term effects of the hit were difficult to overcome. When Justin returned to the lineup, however, he went on a tear for the next three weeks, and by May 11 he had a batting average of .411. During that time, he hit home runs in four consecutive games, and he had two other games in which he had four hits in each game. These were the first four-hit games of his young career.

> *Although he missed only 16 playing days, the long-term effects of the hit were difficult to overcome.*

Justin was upset with Ron Villone. Of course, sometimes batters get hit, but it is courtesy to phone the player later and offer apologies and well wishes. Ron never did that. Justin got even, though. The next time he faced the pitcher was during the heat of the pennant race, on September 2, 2006, more than a year later. Ron was now pitching for the New York Yankees, and with the Twins trailing 1-0, Justin hit a mammoth, three-run home run to lead the Twins to a 6-1 victory! It was a long wait to get back at him, but it was worth it. "That felt pretty good," Justin admitted with a grin. "It was the situation, too. It was a one-run game and I hit a three-run homer, and that was pretty cool."

Most batters will tell you that the most difficult part of making it to the big leagues is the second time through the league. The first time a player goes against teams he has the advantage because no one knows what to expect from the player. His habits are different; his hitting is still a mystery; no one has done much scouting on the player. But when a player faces a team for the second time, the opponents are more prepared. Each team has a full scouting report and knows exactly what the hitter likes to do—hit the ball to one place in the field, or all over; hit the first pitch or never swing at the first pitch; hit for power or happily hit a single; hit inside pitches, or outside, low or high; hit fastballs or curve balls, or have trouble with those pitches. All of the factors that gave a batter the advantage the first time became disadvantages the second time.

> *As always, though, the good players make the necessary adjustments and learn how to ensure their own improvements.*

As always, though, the good players make the necessary adjustments and learn how to ensure their own improvements. In this regard, Justin also learned about the pitchers he would face. He learned which ones threw certain pitches in certain situations, so he could anticipate pitches. He learned which ones had great fastballs or great curveballs, which ones liked to throw inside or outside, high or low. Just as his opponents got to know him better, he also got to know them better. But, of course, this all takes time.

As a result, the rest of the 2005 season was a time of learning for Justin. That .411 average fell slowly and surely the rest of the year, and by the time he had played his final game, on October 2, his average was just .239. To make matters worse, the Twins missed the playoffs for the first time in five years. At the same time, there were some good things to come out of the year for Justin.

Mickey Mantle (left) was one of the original M & M boys.

Justin makes solid contact with a pitch and follows through with a full swing.

First, he had always been perceived as a weak defensive player at first base because this wasn't his natural position. But, in turned out that he played first like he played catcher—thinking all the time about using his skills as a hockey goalie. "In hockey, you just try to knock the puck down," he explained. "I guess at first base...you just knock [the ball] down and keep it close...It's a little bit different at short or third. If you don't field it cleanly, [the runner] will be safe." In 2005, Justin made just eight errors at first base, a pretty good number for someone who had played the position for only a few years.

The other major event that happened in Justin's life in 2005 occurred off the field. Coming into the year, he knew for the first time he would be in Minnesota all season, so he needed to find a home. He teamed up with catcher Joe Mauer, another exciting young player on the team. Joe had a ranch outside of town, and Justin moved there so he could relax and relieve the stress of playing when he wasn't on the field.

> We just pretty much get up, come to the park, go home, watch TV, and go to bed.

"Our house is pretty boring," Justin offered. "We don't really do a whole lot. We just pretty much get up, come to the park, go home, watch TV, and go to bed. On an off day we'll have a barbeque or something, but it's nothing major."

Although the two were good friends and got along well, they had one problem about which they could do very little. Both of their last names started with the letter M, and early in the year one newspaper in Minneapolis nicknamed the pair the M & M boys. On the surface, this sounded kind of funny. It was an obvious reference to the candy, but it was a compliment because only stars and heroes generally get nicknames. The problem was that the nickname was not original; it was a reference to something else. Back in the 1950s, there were two other players named the M & M boys—Mickey Mantle and

The classic swing of Justin Morneau.

Roger Maris of the New York Yankees, only two of the greatest players of all time.

Justin and Joe didn't like the nickname because it implied an expectation that people wanted them to play like Mantle and Maris, a really unfair expectation when the two had so little major league experience by the start of 2005. As Justin honestly said about the M & M nickname, "It was more annoying than flattering, just because of who had the label before us. It's a hall of famer (Mantle) and a guy who held the home-run record for about 40 years (Maris). It's kind of tough. We were coming into our first full season."

As the season wore on, the clubhouse became a less and less happy place. The team was not winning as much as it had expected, and all of the players—veterans, youngsters, pitchers—were not performing to the levels they or their manager had expected. By the end of the season, there were many questions to be answered, but Justin tried to maintain a positive attitude. "Obviously, my confidence is not what it could be," he admitted, "but I try not to worry about that. I just try to have good at-bats...I've struggled more than I'd like to, but I've learned from it—I am learning from it—and I will be better for it next year."

> *"The biggest thing for me was that I didn't have a full winter to work out. I got weak."*

Justin was able to trace the poor season to his inability to prepare during the off-season. "The biggest thing for me was that I didn't have a full winter to work out. I got weak. The first month [of the 2005 season], I was fine, but after that my body started to get tired. That's when I lost a lot of confidence and started doing things I normally don't do at the plate."

Two other factors came into play as well. One, Justin had a sore elbow for much of the year and felt pain every time he swung the bat. Doctors told him the trouble was bone chips, but an operation wasn't necessary so long as he could tolerate the

Justin gets a few congratulations when he gets to the dugout after a big play.

pain. He decided to play through the pain rather than have an operation and miss most of the rest of the season.

The second thing was even more important. The team had lost veteran Corey Koskie during the off-season, and Justin had relied heavily on Corey for advice and guidance during the last half of 2004. Corey was a left-hand batter with a powerful swing, so Justin used to talk to Corey all the time about swing patterns, preparation, and consistency at the plate. All through 2005, the Twins didn't have an experienced, left-handed batter with any power, so Justin was all alone when it came to learning.

He did end the season on a positive note in one way, however. On September 30, 2005, the third-last game of the year, Justin came into the game in the eighth inning and hit his first career grand-slam home run to give the Twins a 7-3 win over Detroit. It was just another sign of what he was capable of doing—he just had to find a way to do it more consistently.

Justin's combination of power and discipline at the plate make him one of the game's best all-'round hitters today.

CHAPTER SEVEN

FROM GOAT TO GLORY

Justin releases the b
on this follow-throu
a three-run home ru
against Kansas City
September 25, 2006

"Justin called me and said, 'Pops,
I got the call. I'm the MVP.'"

George Morneau

Everything was now in place for 2006 to be a great year for Justin. He had played two half seasons and one full season with the Twins; he knew the pitchers, teams, and ballparks; he had a great off-season with a full training schedule. And, even better, the Twins had traded pitcher J.C. Romero to Los Angeles for Alexi Casilla. Why was this important? Because J.C. wore number 33! As soon as the pitcher was traded, Justin called the team and requested Patrick Roy's number, the same number he had tattooed in a maple leaf on one of his shoulders!

But when the regular season started, that optimism was nowhere to be found. Justin went 0-for-4 in the first game of the season, 1-for-5 the next day, and 0-for-3 the day after. More frustrating was that these first three games of 2006 took place in Toronto, the only Canadian stop on tour for the players, and a place where Justin always got extra excited about playing.

> *He was hitting inconsistently, not driving the ball, and not providing much offense for the team.*

He had three hits in his next game to start a three-game series in Cleveland, but then the rest of April was a disaster. By the end of the month he was hitting just .203 despite batting clean-up and playing all but two innings of the team's first 21 games. The month of May was not much better. Justin brought his average up to .244, but that was hardly reason to smile. He was hitting inconsistently, not driving the ball, and not providing much offense for the team. The Twins were just 22-25 through the first two months and 47 games of the season, not nearly good enough if they wanted to get back into the playoffs.

"It's been frustrating," Justin confessed, trying to find an answer for his slump. "It's one of those things where sometimes, when I start feeling good, I swing at too many pitches. I feel so good and I am seeing the ball so well that I can get myself out...

It's one of those things where I have to keep it simple and not try to do too much. I am just trying to be consistent with my at-bats, my approach, and I'll be all right."

Oddly, despite Justin's weak play, he was still one of the best hitters on the team in terms of hits, RBIs, and home runs. He was doing his part in relation to his teammates, but the team as a whole also needed to improve. Things reached a low point on June 7 in Seattle. Manager Ron Gardenhire called Justin into his office for a private meeting. He told the young player that he was capable of doing much more, but that for this game tonight, he would be watching from the dugout and thinking about his game, not playing as he had every day up to that point. It was difficult for Justin to hear this, especially because Justin loved to play in Seattle. This was the city closest to home in British Columbia and one in which he could count on his father attending. It was a meeting that was hard for Justin, but it was a day that changed his life forever.

"It woke me up," Justin said of his life-changing meeting with the manager.

Late in the game that night, Justin got one at-bat in the 11th inning of a 10-9 loss to the Mariners in extra innings. Justin went 1-for-5 the next day, back in the lineup and playing first base, and the next day he had the best game of his career. Justin hit two home runs in four at-bats, had five RBIs, and led the team to a 7-5 home win over the Baltimore Orioles. The day after that he was 3-for-4 with two more RBIs, then 2-for-4 (and another two RBIs), then 3-for-5, and then 2-for-4 with four more RBIs. Justin caught fire, played with enormous confidence, and took the team on his shoulders the rest of the season.

"It woke me up," Justin said of his life-changing meeting with the manager. "He lit a fire under me...There wasn't too much said that was bad or anything. It was just, 'Your focus

Francisco Liriano, a rookie of the year candidate until he got hurt,
is part of a fine young pitching staff in Minnesota.

Justin wearing his favourite number 33.

needs to be on the field. You can do a lot of things in this game that people can't do.' Gardy helped me realize that I can be a lot better than I was. He saw the potential in me, and he cares about his players. It gave me confidence."

It sure did. Prior to the talk, Justin was batting .236 with eleven home runs and 38 RBIs. Between that conversation with Ron Gardenhire and the end of the year, Justin hit .362, had 145 hits including 23 home runs, and contributed 92 RBIs. That .362 average was the best in the majors, as was the RBI total and the total number of hits. On June 7, the Twins were well back in the standings. At the end of the season, they had won the AL Central Division title with a record of 71-33 thanks to Justin's domination after June 7. Overall, Justin batted .321 with 34 homers and 130 runs batted in, and his slugging percentage of .559 was sixth in the AL. He was the first Minnesota player to hit more than 30 homers in a year since 1987, and his 130 RBIs tied Larry Walker for most ever by a Canadian.

> *"He keeps it simple...puts you into a routine and gets you feeling comfortable. I'm pretty happy with the way it's going."*

In addition to the pep talk from his manager, though, two other factors contributed to Justin's revival. First, he started to learn more from the batting coach, Joe Vavra. "He's always positive," Justin said of Joe. "He keeps it simple...puts you into a routine and gets you feeling comfortable. I'm pretty happy with the way it's going." The two also knew each other from the minor leagues, so theirs was a friendship and professional association that went back several years. Justin had faith and trust in Joe, and Joe in turn knew that Justin was a special player capable of special achievements.

The second important factor that helped Justin break out was...a T-shirt. Let Justin explain. "One of my buddies gave [a Vancouver Canucks T-shirt] to me, and I started wearing it in June. We started winning and I started hitting, so I've worn it ever since," he said with a laugh.

The incredible season that Justin put together earned him the American League's most valuable player award, the first time a Canadian in the American League had ever been so honoured. Appropriately, Larry Walker was the only other Canadian named MVP, for the National League in 1997. He didn't waste any time congratulating Justin. "I got a call today from Larry Walker when I was driving into the stadium," Justin revealed during the press conference announcing his MVP win. "He said he just wanted to call and say congrats. He said he was more excited than I was. He said, just wait, it's going to be crazy and just have fun with it. For me to be put next to a guy who, in my opinion, should be put in the hall of fame and is the greatest position player who has ever played...to be alongside him is a real honour."

"I got a call today from Larry Walker when I was driving into the stadium..."

More important, Justin also told how he would talk to Larry when things weren't so happy. "I talked to him and text messaged him at the start of this season when things weren't going so well," Justin acknowledged.

Of course, when he got the news, he also phoned his dad. It was an emotional call, to say the least. "I'm thrilled," said George Morneau. "It's the best day of my life. Justin called me and said, 'Pops, I got the call. I'm the MVP.' And I said, 'unreal.' I started shaking and crying, and all of a sudden he's crying. He said, 'Dad, I have to go and do a news conference.' And I said, 'Go have fun.'"

The MVP vote was very close. Derek Jeter of the New York Yankees and David Ortiz of the Boston Red Sox were the only other players whose names appeared on all 28 ballots. In total, Justin had 320 points, Derek 306, and David 193. The result was expected by Minnesota and its fans, but people in New York and Boston were upset because their top players had better years statistically. For instance, Derek had a batting average of .343 and also stole 34 bases. David had an amazing 54 home runs and 137 RBIs, also better than Justin.

What separated Justin from the other two was that it was clear that when Justin struggled, the whole team struggled, and when he started to play incredibly well, so did the team. In other words, Justin carried the team to the division title, something Derek Jeter and David Ortiz couldn't say with the same proof. Even Justin's opponents agreed. Said Kevin Millar of Baltimore: "As soon as he [Justin] started basically tearing the league apart, the whole team jumped on his back. Morneau has been unbelievable...he means everything in that lineup."

"As soon as he [Justin] started basically tearing the league apart, the whole team jumped on his back."

Minnesota teammate Rondell White, a good friend of Derek Jeter's, agreed. "We wouldn't be here if it wasn't for Justin. He's been carrying us for a while."

In addition to Justin's amazing award, the Twins also had other winners. Joe Mauer—the other half of the M & M boys—won the AL batting title and Johan Santana won the Cy Young Award as the best pitcher in the AL. Francisco Liriano was also on his way to being rookie of the year until he suffered injuries and missed many games. Still, this was a team of award winners.

Unfortunately for the Twins and these stars, the post-season was again unkind to Minnesotans. They were swept aside by the Yankees in three straight games, even though Justin went 5-for-12 with two home runs in the three games. Nonetheless, he had proved in 2006 that he could play as everyone had hoped, even expected. He could hit for average and for power, drive in runs from the all-important fourth spot in the lineup, and carry the team to victory. It seemed only a matter of time before he would be playing in the World Series.

CHAPTER EIGHT

AFTER AN MVP YEAR...?

Justin tags out Michael Young of USA during the World Baseball Classic in 2006. Canada won the game, 8-6.

"Any year of experience ... is key to your development."

Justin

Justin Morneau set a very high standard early in his career by which he would always be judged. He was named the best player in the American League at age 26 after just four years in the majors and only two full seasons. He would always be expected to play as well as that MVP year or risk being called a "one-year wonder" or someone who had a "career year" back in 2006, as if to say that was one lucky season and he really wasn't as good as that year suggested.

Another big change for the now-MVP coming into the 2007 season was his personal life. He had moved out of the farm with his friend Joe Mauer to live in an apartment with his girlfriend, Krista Martin. They had a place together in New Westminster in the off-season, but they wanted to live together year 'round, in Minneapolis during the baseball season, as well.

Before going to training camp with the Twins, Justin had one important appearance to deal with first. Over the course of the previous year, the league and players had arranged a tournament called the World Baseball Classic, featuring 16 national teams from around the world competing in a three-week tournament in March. Of course, Justin was selected to play for Canada, but the Canadians failed to advance past the preliminary round. They lost games to South Africa, 3-2, and Mexico, 9-1, but they did beat the Americans, 8-6. Nevertheless, it was a great experience for Justin especially since his boyhood friend, Jeff Francis, was named to the team as a pitcher. And, Larry Walker, now retired, was one of the coaches and worked every day with the players.

"If he felt like he could help you, he was there to say whatever needed to be said," Justin observed of Larry's role with the team.

> *Another big change for the now-MVP coming into the 2007 season was his personal life.*

Although Canada didn't go as far in the World Baseball Classic as it hoped (Japan beat Cuba 10-6 in the finals), Justin got to the Twins' training camp in excellent condition and ready to play. The season opened on April 2, and Justin almost single-handedly led his team to victory that day. Minnesota beat Baltimore 7-4, and Justin had three hits—including a home run—and three runs batted in. The MVP was off to a great start.

Of course, a season is 162 games long, not just one, so there was plenty of work to do before Justin could take it easy. Over the course of the first month, Justin's average went down and down until it stopped at .271. This was not a bad average by any means—it just wasn't an MVP average. This year, though, both the player and manager weren't going to wait until the middle of the season to tackle this problem. For whatever reason, it seemed Justin was a "slow starter," but the team needed him to play strongly from the beginning of the season.

> *"I think it all stems from a selfless attitude,"* teammate Michael Cuddyer noted.

On May 6, after a 4-3 loss to Boston, Justin and his manager Ron Gardenhire had another meeting. Justin then sat down with batting coach Joe Vavra and together they watched tapes of Justin's swing to determine what he was doing well and what he was doing poorly so they could compare the good habits with the bad tendencies. The next day, Justin went 2-for-5. Both hits were home runs, and he had four RBIs to lead the Twins to a 7-4 win.

"I think it all stems from a selfless attitude," teammate Michael Cuddyer noted. "You could see it last year when this happened. What happens is he puts pressure on himself to get the job done, but when he relies on his teammates and doesn't pressure himself, that's when he gets the job done." Another factor that might have come into play that turned a lousy April

Corey Koskie rounds the bases after a home run for Canada at the World Baseball Classic.

Justin hoists the Stanley Cup on ice with the Anaheim Ducks after the final game in June 2007.

into a superb May was that he was in the process of moving from an apartment to a new house with Krista. No doubt once he was settled he could feel a little more relaxed about his life at home.

Nonetheless, the struggles of 2006 and his talk with manager Ron Gardenhire would always be a constant reminder to Justin about how good he was but how important it was to stay focused every game, every year. "It's something I have to constantly remind myself of," he admitted, "why I'm where I'm at and how quickly it can go away. I know I could quickly go back to being not so good if I didn't do that."

During the last half of May, the Twins had a 10-3 record and Justin started to play like the MVP player he knew he could be. By the end of the month, his play caught the attention of everyone around the league, and he was named Player of the Month in the AL, the first time he had been so honoured. On June 17, Justin rescued the team from the brink of disaster. The Twins had built a comfortable 9-2 lead over Milwaukee, only to see the Brewers rally and tie the game.

> *He had a home run, a double, walked twice, drove in three runs, scored three times, and had a sacrifice fly.*

But in the bottom of the ninth inning, Justin hit a walk-off homer to give the team a dramatic 10-9 win (a walk-off homer is one in which it wins the game and is the last play of the game, so technically the batter doesn't have to run around the bases). It capped a great day for Justin. He had a home run, a double, walked twice, drove in three runs, scored three times, and had a sacrifice fly. All in a day's work!

Indeed, that was his fourth career walk-off home run, two of the previous ones coming in 2007. His first had come on June 9, 2006, against Baltimore. This recent success might have been connected to another, seemingly unconnected event. On June 6, 2007, the Anaheim Ducks won their first Stanley Cup, defeating the Ottawa Senators 6-2 to win the best-of-seven series in five games.

Justin tries a wide slide but is tagged out at the plate by Detroit's Mike Rabelo.

Justin was good friends with Anaheim defenceman Chris Pronger, and Chris invited Justin to the final game. Long after the fans had left the building, the Ducks returned to the ice for a party, and Justin was there, hoisting the Stanley Cup high over his head like a player and drinking champagne from it. Being around these winners could only have helped inspire Justin to bigger and better things when he returned to the ball diamond the next day.

Because of his fantastic play, Justin was named to play in the All-Star Game in 2007 at San Francisco, and he was also asked to participate in the highly popular home-run derby. But before he got to San Francisco, Justin made one more statement about his star status. On July 6, 2007, he hit three home runs in a single game. He had a career-high six RBIs and took the team to an easy 12-0 win over the Chicago White Sox. He was just the fourth member of the Twins in their history to hit three homers in a game, and the first of those hits was the 100th home run of his young career. The blasts gave him 23 on the season, second only to Alex Rodriguez in the American League. He was named player of the week for his fantastic stretch of games leading up to the All-Star break, another first.

Justin had a great time during the All-Star Weekend. He didn't win the Home Run Derby, but he performed well, and in the All-Star Game he went hitless in two at-bats (a line out and a pop up). Despite the great first half of the season, Justin and the team didn't have the same success as in 2006. Justin's average of .271 was well below his MVP year, but he still had 31 home runs and drove in 111 runs, world-class totals by anyone's standards. He was the first Twins player to have consecutive 100-RBI seasons since Gary Gaetti in 1986 and '87.

> *"Anytime you can go out there and play 150-plus games, you learn a lot about yourself."*

Although the Twins didn't make it to the playoffs, Justin could head into the off-season with many good memories. "There are a lot of positives," he said about 2007. "We had two guys drive in 100 runs again. I made my first All-Star team...we had a lot of young pitchers who got some experience. Any year of experience you can get—another 600 at-bats—is key to your development. Anytime you can go out there and play 150-plus games, you learn a lot about yourself."

The truth is, Justin Morneau might have been an MVP in 2006 at age 26, but he had not yet reached his prime. The best has yet to come for this all-star ball star.

JUSTIN MORNEAU: BY THE NUMBERS

Justin Ernest George Morneau

b. New Westminster, British Columbia, May 15, 1981

#33—First Base—Bats left—Throws right

6'4" 223 lbs.

Drafted in 1999 by Minnesota Twins (3rd round, 89th overall)

Minor League Statistics

Year	Team	GP	AB	Runs	Hits	HR	RBI	BB	K	Avg.
1999	TWI	17	53	3	16	0	9	2	6	.302 (1)
2000	ELIZ	6	23	4	5	1	3	1	6	.217 (2)
2000	TWI	52	194	47	78	10	58	30	18	.402 (1)
2001	QCY	64	236	50	84	12	53	26	38	.356 (3)
2001	FTM	53	197	25	58	4	40	24	41	.294 (4)
2001	NBR	10	38	3	6	0	4	3	8	.158 (5)
2002	NBR	126	494	72	147	16	80	42	88	.298 (5)
2003	NBR	20	79	14	26	6	13	7	14	.329 (5)
2003	ROC	71	265	39	71	16	42	28	56	.268 (6)
2004	ROC	72	288	51	88	22	63	32	47	.306 (6)

(1) TWI=GCL Twins (Gulf Coast League, Rookie League)

(2) ELIZ=Elizabethton Twins (Appalachian League, Rookie League)

(3) QCY=Quad City River Bandits (Midwest League, A level)

(4) FTM=Ft. Myers Miracle (Florida State League, A+ level)

(5) NBR=New Britain Rock Cats (Eastern League, AA level)

(6) ROC= Rochester Red Wings (International League, AAA level)

Major League Baseball—American League

Regular Season

Year	Team	GP	AB	Runs	Hits	HR	RBI	BB	K	Avg.
2003	MIN	40	106	14	24	4	16	9	30	.226
2004	MIN	74	280	39	76	19	58	28	54	.271
2005	MIN	141	490	62	117	22	79	44	94	.239
2006	MIN	157	592	97	190	34	130	53	93	.321
2007	MIN	157	590	84	160	31	111	64	91	.271
Career		569	2,058	296	567	110	394	198	362	.276

Playoffs

Year	Team	GP	AB	Runs	Hits	HR	RBI	BB	K	Avg.
2004	MIN	4	17	1	4	0	2	0	3	.235
2006	MIN	3	12	3	5	2	2	0	0	.417
Career		7	29	4	9	2	4	0	3	.310

MIN= Minnesota Twins

World Baseball Classic, March 3-20, 2006

Year	Team	GP	AB	Runs	Hits	HR	RBI	BB	K	Avg.
2006	CAN	3	13	3	4	0	2	2	4	.308

CAN= Canada

Legend:
GP=game splayed
AB=at bats
HR=home runs
RBI=runs batted in
BB=base on balls
K=strikeouts
Avg.=batting average

Glossary

assist   throw the ball to a teammate to make an out

at-bat   an official appearance at the plate (not counting walks or sacrifices)

bag   one of three bases in the field (first, second, third)

balk   a move by a pitcher toward home plate while throwing, usually, to first base (illegal)

ball   a pitch outside the strike zone; the object used to throw and hit in baseball

base hit   a hit by a batter which allows him to advance at least as far as first base without a defensive error

base on balls   four balls, entitling the batter to go to first base

bases loaded   situation in which one team has runners on all three bases

batter's box   area defined by white chalk in which the batter must stand to hit the ball

battery   the combination of catcher and pitcher

box score   game summary for a baseball game

breaking ball   pitch which moves radically, fooling the batter

bullpen   area of the ballpark where all pitchers can warm up

bunt   short touch of the ball with the bat intended to advance a runner or fool the defence, allowing the batter to get to first base

catcher   defensive player who stands behind home plate and works with the pitcher

caught looking   strikeout in which the batter watches the third strike (as opposed to swinging for a strikeout)

change-up   slower pitch than a fastball designed to fool the batter

check swing   swing by the batter which he tries to stop the swinging motion, but too late

chopper   hard hit ball into the ground near home plate, resulting in a high bounce

clean-up   batter who hits fourth in the lineup

closer   final relief pitcher who enters a game usually in the ninth inning to make the final out(s) for a victory

complete game   nine full innings, usually used to describe a pitcher who lasts the entire game

count   the number of balls and strikes in an at-bat, as recorded by the umpire

curveball   pitch which drops radically as it approaches the plate, fooling the batter

cycle (hit for) hit a single, double, triple, and home run in the same game

designated hitter player who hits but does not play defence (used only in the American League; in the National League the pitcher always bats)

diamond playing field

double two-base hit in which the batter advances to second base after hitting the ball without a defensive error

double-header two games played between the same two teams on the same day

double play defensive play in which two outs are recorded on the same play

dugout area where players not participating in the game can sit

earned run run scored without error

error mistake which allows a batter to reach base or advance after a play which usually results in a put-out

fair ball ball which lands inside the chalk lines marking the playing field

fastball the fastest possible pitch a pitcher can throw

fielder's choice defensive play in which a player other than the hitter running to first is put out (the batter reaches base but is not credited with a hit because he would reasonably have been put out had the fielder decided to attempt the put out)

fly ball ball hit in the air to the outfield

force out play in which the batter hits the ball but a teammate already on base is thrown out as a result of the hit

forkball pitch which dips wildly, crazily, and unpredictably, fooling the batter

foul ball ball which lands outside the chalk lines marking the playing field

grand slam home run hit while the bases are loaded

ground ball ball hit along the ground to one of the infielders, usually resulting in an out

hit by pitch batter who is hit by a pitch and is allowed to go to first base as a result

home plate spot inside the batter's box with one pointed end and one flat end, the object of which is to touch home plate to score a run and over which the pitcher must throw the ball for a strike to be called

home run hit which allows the batter to run around all four bases to score a run

infielder one of four defensive positions around the bags (first base, second base, third base, shortstop)

infield hit hit ball which never gets through the infield, in which no error is made, but in which the batter advances to first base

inning three outs per side

intentional walk pitcher who throws four balls to a batter with the intention of allowing him to reach first base

knuckleball very slow pitch without any twist or turns to the ball, making it very difficult to hit

left on base players who remain on base once three outs have been made (referred to as LOB in box scores)

line drive hard hit that never goes far off the ground

mound hill 60'6" from home plate from which the pitcher throws the ball

no-hitter complete game in which a pitcher does not allow a single hit

outfield area beyond the infield guarded by three positions (left fielder, right fielder, centre fielder)

passed ball pitch which goes back past the catcher which he reasonably should have caught

perfect game game in which a pitcher makes 27 consecutive outs, not allowing one batter on base for any reason

pick off throw by the pitcher to a base (usually first base) which catches a runner by surprise and causes an out

pinch hitter hitter who comes into the game to replace a player

pinch runner runner who comes into the game to replace a player

pitchout throw by the pitcher to the catcher but which is intentionally outside the strike zone, making it easy for the catcher to catch (usually when they think a runner is going to try to steal a base)

pull hitter hitter who generally hits the ball to the same side he bats (i.e., a left-handed batter hits to right field most times)

rubber that strip of rubber on the pitcher's mound

run any time a player crosses home plate to score

run batted in a hit by the batter which brings a run home to score (except when the hitter hits into a double play)

runner offensive player who assumes a place on one of the bases, hoping to score

sacrifice bunt bunt by a batter which is intended only to advance a teammate from first base to second or second base to third

sacrifice fly fly ball hit by the batter which is deep enough to allow a runner to advance from second base to third or to score from third base

safe call by an umpire to declare a runner's status

save successful appearance by a relief pitcher to preserve a win started by another pitcher

scoring position runner who is on either second base or third base

shortstop defensive player situated between the second baseman and third baseman

signal hand gesture by a catcher to tell the pitcher what kind of pitch to throw (fastball, slider, etc.)

sinker fast pitch that drops sharply as it reaches home plate

slider fast pitch that moves down just before a batter is about to hit it

steal run from first to second or second to third during the time a pitcher throws the ball from the mound to home plate

strike call by an umpire to declare a pitch is within the strike zone

strike out batter's failed attempt to hit the ball before having three strikes called against him

strike zone that area over home plate between a batter's knees and waist in which a strike will be called by the umpire

suicide squeeze bunt by a batter while a runner from third base is racing toward home plate

switch hitter batter who can hit from either side of the plate, depending on whether the pitcher is left-handed or right-handed

tag touch a runner with the ball before he reaches a base, resulting in an out

tag-up run from one base to another after a fielder has caught the ball to make an out on the batter

triple three-base hit in which the batter advances to third base after hitting the ball without a defensive error

triple play one single play which results in three outs

umpire judge of play, of which there are four for every game (one for each base)

walk batter who is able to make the pitcher throw four balls, allowing the batter to go to first base

walk-off homer home run to end a game

wild pitch pitch by a pitcher toward the catcher who has little chance of blocking it before the ball goes astray

Photo Credits

All photos are courtesy of Reuters

Acknowledgements

The author would like to thank publisher Jordan Fenn for his ongoing support of this program which has now produced six books. Also, to Michael Gray at First Image, the designer for the series, and to my agent Dean Cooke. Finally, a special thanks to my wife, Emma Grace, for all her support, even though baseball isn't her number-one sport!

For More Information

Baseball is a sport rich in history, some in stories, most in statistics. Here are a select few websites to visit for more information, more detailed statistics, and additional details about Justin Morneau:

www.justinmorneau.com

www.sportspic.com

www.baseball-almanac.com

http://minors.baseball-reference.com

http://morneau.davidzingler.com

http://www.thebaseballcube.com

http://www.sportspic.com/cndsports/cndmlb.htm

http://www.baseballhalloffame.ca/